OPERATE A SUCCESSFUL DAY CARE IN YOUR HOME

****

by "Ms. Ellen"

1stBooks - rev. 1/3/02

DEDICATION

To my husband Bill who allowed me to dedicate many hours in this adventure and to my children Billy, Peggy, Kathy, Kimberly and Demetra who taught me most everything there is to know about children. Also to all the day care providers who dedicate themselves in the rearing of children.

PREFACE

Ellen Saunders first started baby sitting as a teenager. She played games and read many stories to children.

After high school she married and raised five children of her own. During the years she gave many babies their first mouth full of real food for rookie parents. Also she guided many young parents with child care just as she had been guided as a young parent.

Her children call often to discuss what is going on in the life of her little ones.

Ellen has been caring for children on and off for over forty years. She has operated her own day care for the last twenty years. Ellen is devoted and very caring toward people.

The information is this book is not so much on how to care for children as there are many books on the market catering to child care. Here she relates to unusual situations and how to handle them.

The book is written in a language that anyone who can read will understand. No large vocabulary or astronomical phrases. Simple down to earth wording.

In her spare time Ellen loves to sing, play the guitar, and enjoys her grandchildren.

"Ms. Ellen" resides in Williamsburg, Virginia.

CONTENTS CHAPTER   PAGE

INTRODUCTION
by Bill Saunders

It was the year 1971. My wife Ellen and I had bought a home in Rockville Maryland. Two of our five children were in school and the other three at home. Costs on groceries and other products were steadily on the increase. Then came the lettuce boycott and the gasoline crunch, when prices sky rocketed in some cases more than 100%. The change in the economy was a shock and certainly was not expected.

Needing more income to adjust meant that Ellen may need to get into the working world. She went through being a waitress, a computer operator and working with the school system.

There were numerous times when her relief did not show up or last minute work came about. This meant that no one could be at home when the kids got out of school. There was a need also to take off from work, when the school called, do to a sick child or a need to stay at home if one of the children were sick. With five children it seemed as if one of them were at home quite often.

After paying someone to look after the pre-school children, providing extra transportation for Ellen to work and in furnishing uniforms or clothes to work in, the additional income was not beneficial.

Ellen told me that she thought it would be best if she were to stay at home to take care of the children as her working a job was costing more then if she were not in the working world. In addition, someone would be at home when the children were dismissed from school. There was no question about it, as we both agreed, for the sake of the children and our sanity.

Back to square one. High monthly expenses, but not enough monthly income. As the saying goes there was too much month left over at the end of the money.

Then Ellen comes up with a brain storm. She was going to baby sit. Oh sure, five kids and she's going to take on more. I desperately attempted to talk her out of this. She insisted that at least lets give it a try. If it didn't work she could discontinue doing it.

Well, she gave it a try. Some income was earned and expenses were lowered. We were getting by. She had taken in a couple of full timers and a couple of drop ins. This was about all that could be handled along with our own children. There were also obstacles with having "strangers" in the house, such as how to handle our childrens' eating habits, what toys could be played with and in giving our children the attention that we felt they needed. These obstacles were worked out and the bills were paid.

This continued until two of our children graduated from high school and the younger ones became teenagers.

We relocated to Virginia do to a job change. Then the youngest ones graduated from high school and went on to college.

Now here is Ellen, at home, no children, and few people to communicate with as we had not yet accumulated many friends in the area. She needed to get out and be a part of something to occupy all this lonesome time in which there was plenty of.

Ellen went back to being a waitress and also tried working with a large chain grocery store. Being unable to call the shots when working (in the real world) for other people, she found that after all of these years, it would be very difficult to make adjustments.

Sooo—What about doing a little baby sitting. After all the children were gone and more than two full timers could be taken care of. At least easily up to the number of children that were in the house when our children were at home.

The experience was there, the need was there and there were no obstacles. —Go for it!—

This she did and for the past twenty years she has run a very successful operation, boosted our income tremendously, taught others how to operate and decided that she would like to tell the world.

Here it is, straight from "Ms. Ellen".

AUTHORS NOTES

There has been for many years (and still are) a need for Day Care Providers thoughout the Nation. There also have been many books written on taking care of infants, pre-schoolers, and school age children. Check the shelves in any book store and they are loaded with guidance manuals and babysitting or childcare manuals.

This manual takes a different approach to the operation of a Day Care Business. Along with taking care of children there are other aspects to operating a business. As we take a tour through the manual, together, we find other facts of knowledge are needed to be successful in operating a Day Care.

My first years were stressful and at times, I thought that taking care of kids was not what I wanted to do. As time progressed I learned the tricks of the trade, what makes it successful and how to handle very difficult situations. I also learned how to "MAKE MONEY" in my operation, which is not something the Child Care Guidance books on the store shelves tell you.

First off why are you considering doing Day Care? Could it be that you love children? Could it be so that you can meet new people? Could it be that you would like to see children raised properly? Could it be that you feel you owe something to society? It could be all of the above and than some. However, we all think about our job as the reason we are doing it, is "TO MAKE MONEY".

There will be excerpts from my years in dealing with children. No actual names will be mentioned and incidents can be related to numerous persons or children that at one time were under my care. However no one has been singled out and these occurrences have happened numerous of times over the years.

"My Children" who I have attended to over the years still come back to see me, send me cards, and keep in touch. They also inform me of the many things that they learned about dealing with children while under my care. Some have even helped me in caring for younger children. Many now have children of their own. I feel a great sense of satisfaction that I literally raised many children and also from the appreciation that I have received from the parents. My files are filled with letters of recommendations and appreciations.

As a provider one should provide a safe day care that supports the physical, intellectual, emotional and discipline needs of the child.

I recommend that if you are going to take care of children that you make every attempt to do it with their future being taken into consideration (in growth). I also strongly recommend that your future be taken into consideration (financially).

In your area there is a Childrens Support Group or a similar guidance organization. Join it and be an active participant. They will keep you updated on new requirements, refer persons to you who need day care, provide workshops to assist in gaining knowledge and they will take an interest in your operation.

Some state colleges or Social Services offer free credited courses on child development that day care providers are eligible to attend.

This book is written in phases and by chapter, so that you may refer to the section needed upon situations that may arise. I suggest that you take notes as you go along so that you may relay thoughts to the parents during the initial interview. There is also a question and answer chapter for reference.

The one thing which needs to be emphasized is that most children are not a problem after your break-in period. However you will need to learn how to communicate with the parents. They will put you in many more difficult situations than the kids will. It is most important for you that the parents will work with you.

There's a right way, a wrong way, your way and my way. Lets get started and learn how to help children and "TO MAKE MONEY" doing it my way.

GETTING STARTED

Most Day Care Providers would rather stay small and work out of their homes. There is little or no costs in starting out in this manner. Also, if this is a first time experience for you, it is recommended that this be the way to go.

To begin you will need space such as a spare room, a basement, a garage or a fairly good size yard. Make these areas safe and provide a few safe toys, which are appropriate for the age group you plan to care for.

The easiest way to get started is in talking to people and let them know what you plan to do. Decide what hours you intend to work and stick to those requirements. More on this later.

You can post notices on bulletin boards in drug stores, libraries, and grocery stores in your area.(Page 79) You can run a small ad in your community paper. Join a Child Support Group. They will keep your profile on record and make referrals to you for persons seeking day care. Notify the schools of your intentions. Keep talking as word of mouth is the surest way for parents to hear about your interests.

The Child Support group may require that you have a criminal background check, a fire inspection of your home and a TB screen test. They will assist you with the proper forms and the costs are no more than a doctors visit. (Tax deductibles)

Most parents will need someone from 7:00 a.m. to 5:30 p.m. This is a long day and without help, no breaks or dilly dally time for you. As time goes on you will be able to make adjustments, but for now we are just getting started. On this job you will have major holidays and weekends off.

Getting started is not difficult and not much attention needs to be given to this area as all the facets, which would be included are in their individual chapters.

Record keeping will be of most importance as you will learn in a later chapter. Household expenses are certainly going to go up in the use of electric, water, heating fuel, T paper, etc. It is important to keep receipts and canceled checks so at the end of the year you can deduct percentages of the totals on your tax forms. Also a record of income should be kept for three reasons. One so that you will know how your are progressing, two so that you can tell each parent at the end of the year how much they paid you (if they ask), and thirdly for reporting your income on your federal and state income tax forms. (a must)

Make record keeping simple. Just get a composition or notebook. Keep a page or a separate book for each customer and keep a page to list expenses. When purchasing anything related to day care keep the receipts and a written record, such as, this book you are reading and the books for your record keeping. See - expenses are starting to mount already.

Have business cards made. This will make you look and feel professional. After all, this is what you are now. (Page 79)

As you progress with your business more expenses will be encountered. You may need to purchase some toys, advertise, pay additional help, use your car if transporting, or pay for professional services. You may even decide to purchase a passenger van.

If you want to go big time you may seek money from a bank, from the small business administration, personal friends, investors or you may have other resources. To do this you will need a written plan of the operation of your business financial information as to profit and loss projected over a few years, reliable professional references and possibly some collateral. Also you may need a lawyer, a banker, and a certified public accountant. In my twenty five years as a provider, a lawyer has not been needed. Then, however I never decided to go big time.

My intentions in writing this booklet is for one to start out small time in the home. If one desires later to progress into a larger operation outside of the home, that's up to them.

The home business encounters different methods and values. You, personally, are in direct contact with the children and the parents. It is not a company, it is your business to operate as you see fit, in accordance with the state and county codes, and you set your own standards.

You will need to obtain a business license from your county for a small fee. This makes you legal and they know who to send forms to for taxation purposes.

Check the requirements for a day care permit. This may not pertain to you pending on how many children you plan to keep. There are child care ordinances that exist in most state counties. A certain number of children may be kept without this permit. Checking county regulations will confirm what you may need.

You may be limited to the number of children that you can offer care to, however the procedures and recommendations in this book will remain the same.

OK, now you have an ad in the newspaper and a parent calls to find out about your operation. After you have been at this for a while and with some experience behind you the information that you need to give out will be easy. For now you are new and just starting out. I'm sure that sometime in your lifetime you have baby sit for others or you may even had children of your own. At any rate after using this booklet and your experiences the answers will come.

A parent who calls is of course concerned about the well being of their child. This is good and you are also going to be concerned about the childs well being. Maybe even more so than some parents.

The parent would like it if you would suggest an interview in your home, so that you may explain your operation and so that the parent can see for themselves what your accommodations are. NOTE: I said, "Your operation". This is your business and you run it appropriately. Do not let the parents dictate to you that their child must take a nap from 10:00 to 11:00 and must eat his lunch at 11:30, etc. You set your standards, tell the parents what they are and refrain from changing. So you lose one once in a while, you'll never miss them; but try to accommodate ten parents wishes and you are in for a nervous breakdown. Did you ever ask the movie theater to start the motion picture later just for you? The parent says that you only take care of children until 5:30, but they can't pick up their child until 6:00. Sorry, my work day ends a 5:30 p.m. You'll have enough trouble with late comers. (Later)

Now that you have shown the parent your place of business and the parent shows interest, break out a contract for them to review. (Remember the parent may wish to check other sources. This shows the sign of a concerned parent and you should encourage this) Go over the contract with them thereby you will cover any tracks that may have been missed during the interview. Also give them a form to fill out on the childs information relating to the mother, father, guardian, doctor, or who to contact in an emergency, etc. Let them take it home to complete it. Attempt to establish a date in which they will contact you. The paper work here also serves to show your client that you are business minded and professional. This is not something usually found in someone who is baby sitting.

Remember to set the interview time when you will be able to SIT and TALK with the parents. Preferably a time when you have few or no children. You don't need interruptions or problems to deal with during the interview. You need to concentrate on explaining your operation and the concerns of the parents. If necessary, have a helper to care for the children, while you are tending to business or have the interview after working hours.

When inviting a parent for the interview tell them to bring the child. Also tell them not to mention baby sitting or child care to the child. Let the youngster think the parent is merely making a visit. This way the child will be more relaxed and will more easily become accustomed to the facility. Let the child play at his discretion with the toys or other children. If he thinks this is just a visit he may not be as shy as if he thought that he was going to stay here.

Listen closely for clues, such as, why this person is looking to day care. Was their child in another facility prior to coming to you? Do as much screening as you can. If possible check with the previous provider. Understand that there are personality clashes and if the client and previous provider could not agree, possibly they both learned something from the ordeal and you may benefit with a new customer.

After being in business for a while you will communicate with other providers on a regular basis.

RATES

Before taking in children we need to set or establish a going rate as to what we are to charge. Find out the rates in your area, either from other day care providers or contact the Child Support Group in your area. Below are some weekly rates as samples:

Full time children 7:30 to 5:30, three years and up 95.00

Kindergarten children, half day 50.00

Preschool three days a week 50.00

Preschool two days a week 35.00

Before and after school 40.00

Before school only 25.00

After school only 25.00

Children not under contract (drop in children) are $ 3.50 per/hr with a minimum $ 5.00 fee. This can be rephrased to be $5.00 for the first hour and than $ 3.50 for each hour thereafter.

When children under contract are not in school the charge will be at the daily rate of $ 19.00 per/day for each child.

Some providers take in only infants at $ 70.00 to $ 100.00 per week. This is not covered in this book.

After establishing a rate for the child in which is coming into your day care operation, insert it on the contract prior to letting the parent take the contract. The signed contract is to be returned to you along with the deposit and the first weeks advance fee. This way there will be no question later or "I thought you said". In writing it is established and can only be changed by you. The rate that is established is guaranteed to you whether the child comes or not. You have reserved a space for this child. Parents will agree to this or not accept your services. OK bye, this eliminates having problems latter, almost. There will always be the parent who says, "Joey couldn't come Wednesday, do I have to pay for that day?" This is where you need to be assertive and say, "Yes you do, that space is reserved for Joey and I could not fill it on such short notice." This is one of the biggest mistakes day care providers make. They let the parent slide. Don't do it, as it may become habit forming.

Establish a relatively high fee should a parent want you to keep the child after normal working hours, (sometimes), if permitted by you. In time you will probably make enough that you will not want overtime work. For example using the above rates suppose you care for:

Four full time children at $ 95.00 per week.....................$ 380.00

Five before and after school at 40.00 per week 200.00

Two before school only at 25.00 per week...........................50.00

Two after school only at 25.00 per week..............................<u>50.00</u>

$ 680.00

That's six hundred and eighty dollars per week. Nothing to sneeze at and you're just getting started.

The before and after school children usually arrive at your house at 7:00 a.m. or after and catch the school bus at 8:30. They return from school at 4:00 p.m. and leave prior to 5:30. They are under your care for only three hours. Easy three hundred dollars. In time you may desire to carry more children.

Some day care providers handle only before and after school children. That way they still have their day free.

The full time children come anytime after seven and leave anytime prior to five thirty. This constitutes a full day.

Drop in children may be taken until you have the opportunity to fill that spot with a full time child. After the spot is filled and you are at your predetermined limit, any drop in parents will need to be told that your quota is filled, Sorry, no vacancies. Word travels and than the parents learn that you do not play games. They will cease challenging you and ask for a regular spot.

No cut rates for a family with two or three children. They pay the going rate for each child.

Have all parents make a deposit of $ 60.00 in advance along with the first weeks payment, also in advance. This will help should anyone skip out on you.

This set fee is better than a week in advance money as in time a number of your children will change days, hours, etc. and a weeks advance will be complicated to keep track of. Especially after a year has gone by. However a $ 60.00 fee for all will be easy to remember.

Tell your clients that you expect a check or cash on Friday. Friday is your pay day. They would not like it if they did not receive their pay as scheduled. Should one say, "I left my checkbook at home, but if you need it I will go and get it." Say O.K. and let them go get it. You won't have this problem with this person again. Should any start getting slack about paying on Friday, request your payment to be made on Thursday. Tell them Friday at 5:30 is too late for you to do any bank business or be frank and tell them some people have trouble remembering to make payment on Friday. Let them wonder who.

Tell the parents that a good way to remember the check is to put it in the childs' lunch box when preparing their meal.

Assertiveness is the way you get your money and get it on time. Speak up, if you can't you had better find another field to get into in which one does not have to deal with people.

In effect, what I am getting at, as you can probably see at this point is that the parents are most of the problems that you will encounter. Not the kids, they are easy. More to come on dealing with parents.

Let me point out a very important aspect here. Your business conducted with each client is personal, just the same as business with your doctor or lawyer. Keep business relationships confidential with your clients at all times. You owe them this as a professional.

Children need to unload to someone about problems at home that they are bothered by and don't know how to express themselves. You are the most likely person that they have complete confidence in and they will tell you of family stories, problems, fights, and concerns. They may be true or untrue. With a small child you never know. With experience you can see tell tale signs when the parent comes to pick up the child. You will need to use discretion as to whether to inform the parent of the childs concerns. Again you owe it to your clients to keep such controversies confidential.

CONTRACT

Establish a contract so that an agreement is understood and can be referred to later should any questions arise. It is best to be as thorough as possible leaving no stone unturned. Always keep a blank or spare on hand for copying. I have two contracts, one for the school year and one for summer operations. Here is a copy of one of the contracts that I use:

****
****
****

CHILD CARE CONTRACT

STANDARDS:

Day care hours are between 7:00 a.m. and 5:30 p.m. Monday thru Friday.

Day care is provided for children on a regularly established schedule.

Once a schedule is established payment is required. Whether the child is in attendance or not.

The established fees will be in effect for the duration of this contract, unless there is a change in schedule, in which a new contract will be established.

Drop in children are accepted when a vacancy allows and at the drop in fee.

A sixty dollar advance deposit along with the first weeks advance payment is required.

The day care provider will have the following holidays off with pay:

New Years Day, Memorial Day. Independence Day, Labor Day, Thanksgiving and Christmas Day.

MEALS:

Parents will provide meals, snacks, and drinks.

When a childs lunch is not provided there will be a $3.00 charge for provider to prepare a lunch. NOTE: The provider will not prepare lunches on a regular basis.

TRIAL:

It is agreed that a two-week adjustment period will exist before regular care is established.

HEALTH/ILLNESS AND EMERGENCIES:

Medicines will not be administered to a child without consent of the parent. Please use judgement; do not send your child with a fever or a contagious disease. If your child should become ill during the day you will be notified immediately and will be expected to have the child picked up as soon as possible. Children who become ill may be isolated from the other children. I must have phone numbers where parents can be reached at all times; also, the number of a personal physician. These numbers are to be kept updated. Please notify me as soon as possible when you find your child has a contagious disease so that parents of other children may respond accordingly.

RECREATION:

During the summer season we attend picnics, movies and go to the neighborhood pool on a regular basis. There is a $ 50.00 mandatory pool fee if the child is not already a member of the pool. Recreation outing money must be provided for the child when needed. No personal toys are to be brought without advanced authorization.

CLOTHING:

The childs dress should be so that they may exercise full play. Outdoor play is permitted year round. A change of clothes left with the provider will be helpful in the event the child needs a change.

TRANSPORTATION:

Parents are responsible for transporting their children to and from the day care.

Arrangements may be made with the school transportation system for your child to use a school bus in this area.

Children when traveling in my vehicle will be in approved car seats and/or will be required to use seat belts.

Children may only be picked up by their parents, unless previous arrangements have been made.

BACKUPS:

In the event I have personal business and/or appointments I will provide a experienced qualified sitter in my home during the time period that I am away.

AGREEMENT:

Contract is in agreement until June 30.

Withdrawal of child from day care is acceptable with a two weeks advanced notice.

Contract will become void should the provider discontinue day care services.

Signature verifies that the parent has read and understands the conditions of this contract.

"Ms. Ellen"

Your child _____ will be provided
day care on:
(Circle days)

MONDAY   TUESDAY   WEDNESDAY
THURSDAY   FRIDAY

The rate for _____ will be $ _____ per week.

Signature _____
_____ Date _____

****
****
****

The following is a sample of information and permission to
render care to a child in the event of emergency"

CHILD INFORMATION FOR DAY CARE PROVIDER

CHILDS NAME _____

NICKNAME _____

CHILDS SCHOOL _____

PHONE _____

CHILDS HOME ADDRESS _____

14

_____
_____

HOME PHONE_____

MOTHERS NAME_____

WORK PHONE_____

FATHERS NAME_____

WORK PHONE_____

DOCTORS NAME_____

PHONE_____

IN AN EMERGENCY, IF PARENTS CANNOT BE CONTACTED, NOTIFY:
NAME_____PHONE_____

PREFERRED
HOSPITAL_____

INSURANCE
COMPANY_____

POLICY NO._____
KNOWN   ALLERGIES
_____
_____

COMMENTS_____
_____
_____

"Ms. Ellen"

WE GIVE OUR CONSENT FOR THE ABOVE NAMED DOCTOR OR STAFF OF ABOVE NAMED HOSPITAL TO USE THEIR JUDGMENT IN ADMINISTERING THE REQUIRED MEDICAL ATTENTION DEEMED NECESSARY BY THEM IN CASE NEITHER PARENT CAN BE REACHED.

YES_____ NO_____

<u>PLEASE HAVE NOTARIZED IF THE ABOVE IS CHECKED YES.</u>

DATE_____

PARENT SIGNATURE

_____

PARENT SIGNATURE

_____

SWORN TO AND SUBSCRIBED BEFORE ME THIS _____th DAY OF_____1999.

WITNESS MY HAND AND OFFICIAL SEAL.

_____
_____,

NOTARY PUBLIC
(Signature)

My commission expires:_____,
NOTARY PUBLIC

STANDARDS AND REASONS

Lets rehash parts of the contract and understand why these standards need to be set.

Hours:

Need to be consistent and to coincide with the majority of working persons. This is important to you to obtain your clientele. In addition you are setting yourself up for a routine in which you can handle both mentally and physically. Set your hours and stick to them, regardless of other peoples wishes. Remember this is YOUR operation and you want to do it to make money and not be over worked. A regularly established schedule allows you to schedule other commitments as you know what days your clients are going to be at your place of business.

Payment—

Once a schedule is established payment is required whether the child is in attendance or not. This serves mainly three purposes. One, if the parent is wishy washy about bringing their child they will not want to pay for care that they do not receive and will drop in on you at random. Suppose you had several people doing this. You would lose control. You definitely need to be in complete control at all times. Two, if a child missed periodically you would have a void space that is not producing. Thirdly, you are in this to make money.

There are two periods that do get difficult. These are during your vacation and the vacation of the parents. Most people get anywhere from one to four weeks vacation a year. How are you going to handle this? My suggestion is this. Chances are that they are getting paid for their vacation time by their company, so, why shouldn't you get paid for your vacation? Or, you could establish a back up sitter, or someone who helps you out and knows your routine to watch the children in your home while your are on vacation. You would still receive the weekly payment from your clients and you could pay your back up so much an hour regardless of the number of children. Should you go this route take all phone numbers with you and talk with the stand-in provider at least twice a day. Should the provider have had problems that are in need of attention you than can call the parent. This tells the parents that you stay on top of things, and you will gain even further respect.

As for the parents taking their vacations, it is difficult for people to take a vacation and pay for day care also. I might give them a weeks break and tell them to enjoy themselves. What ever you do be certain that your standard is written into the contract.

Remember the above contract is only a sample. You are not bound by it. Make your own contract using the above as a guide.

Holidays—

Relatively simple to understand. The day care provider will have the following holidays off with pay: New Years Day, Memorial Day, Independence Day, Labor Day, Thanksgiving and Christmas Day.

It is recommended that the Day Care provider be available for all the other holidays as they are not recognized by private industry or by the school system. After all you are providing a service and making money. On the smaller holidays most children will be at home with their parents. Remember you are getting paid whether they are in attendance or not but you must be available to them. Some will bring the children to you because they have to work or they can't adjust to the fact that you are getting paid something for nothing. I venture to say that they are getting paid by their company while they are off.

Adjustments—

The contract is binding so far as we are concerned and is for the duration of the current fiscal year. However, there are circumstances beyond ones control. A person may be reassigned another work schedule at their place of business. It would be gracious of you to adjust your contract as to the change of days as necessary.

Meals/Snacks—

Parents will provide lunches, snacks, and drinks. I have had people drop their children off without a lunch or snack. I in turn will call them at their place of business and request that they bring their child something to eat or I can charge them a fee for lunch. (You could throw together a peanut butter and jelly sandwich for the child).

Make sure that the food the parents bring is already prepared, sandwiches made, soups in micro-wavable containers, etc. Do not let parents pack a can of beans or the like for you to open and cook. Again you are not preparing food or cooking. You do Day Care Work..

There are day care operators that will prepare meals and some receive assistance for this. They cannot take on as many children or would not be able to give the children as much quality time. They may also need to charge considerably more, grocery shop (on their own time) and plan meals accordingly. (Again on their own time).

You on the other hand will know your hours, know that your income is yours, and can live a little personal life.

Trial—

Regular care can be established after a two week trial period. The first two weeks are the hardest for a child to adjust to his new surroundings and to his new friends. Adjustments also consist of your rules and regulations. Most children learn very quickly from you and his peers. Kids have a way of straightening new people out. "Miss Ellen, Georgie is not eating his sandwich." "He's not following the rules." This two week period is also a test to see if you and the child will be compatible. If not then you have an out and can tell the parents frankly that it will not work.

Health—

You are not a doctor and do not attempt to be one. Law suits are forever on the rise for any misdemeanor. Make it a policy that you will not give a child medicine of any kind (including aspirin) without the consent of the parent.

Remind the parents that you will not allow children to be at your place of business with a fever or contagious disease. You are offering the other children the same protection that you would offer this child.

If a child becomes sick he will be isolated from the other children and the parent will be called. The parent will make arrangements to have the child picked up as soon as possible. Tell the parent, "I will be looking for you within the hour."

You must have phone numbers where parents can be reached at all times, also, numbers of their personal physicians.

Periodically check with the parents to see if there are any number changes.

Tell the parents to please notify you as soon as possible when they learn that their child has contacted a contagious disease. This is important so that other parents can be notified and make arrangements to see their childs physician, if necessary.

Recreation—

Plan some sort of activity that all will enjoy and that will take up a considerable amount of time during the day. This is particularly important during the summer season. It is here that you will have more children as the older brothers and sisters of your regular day care children will be out of school for the summer. Parents as a rule like to keep their children together. This will make you much extra money during the summer. You may even consider getting additional help. The days will be full and long.

My time consuming recreation is the use of a neighborhood pool. After the children have been trained to abide by your standards children will not pose a problem to you or to the pool attendants. Sometimes we go twice a day. On the second trip I have the parents pick up their children at the pool prior to 5:30 p.m.

One of the stipulations for children under my care for the summer is that they be members of the pool. Many families are members, but for those that are not there is a pool fee for the summer. This is explained to the parent wishing to enter your summer program and is included in your summer contract. Any parent who does not wish to participate is found out early on and can decide in advance whether they wish their child to be included. They also at this time may decide to go somewhere else. If so let it be. You have a business to operate within your guidelines.

Parents are also informed at the interview that during the summer we will be attending movies. It is a part of your operation. At the beginning I collect five dollars from each childs parent. This money is used on days that I decide to take the children on an outing.

We may go out to lunch or to the movies. Keep this on hand at all times for unexpected schedule changes. Only do this periodically,. such as during inclement weather. Doing it to often can get rather expensive for the parents.

The children may be taken to the library every couple of weeks. Each has his own library card and can check out five books. It is best that you retain the books at your place for the duration of the checkout. This is to utilize the time for your day care and to eliminate book losses.

During the warmer months we take our lunches and go on a picnic to one of the community recreation centers for a few hours of outside activities and exercise. This changes the childrens surroundings and keeps them interested, preventing boredom.

Clothing—

Children pay hard and have accidents of all sorts. They some how manage to find the only mud puddle on twenty square acres of land or miss their mouth when having their juice at snack time. Some providers will laundry the childrens clothes, some will probably let the child go wet. Yuck! Some will recommend an additional set of clothes be left in a bag with the childs name on the bag. This is the least time consuming method as you simply put the soiled clothes in the bag and give them to the parent at pick up time.

Transportation—

Parents are responsible in getting the children to your place of business and likewise in making arrangements to have the child picked up prior to quitting time, 5:30 p.m.

With written permission from the parent to the school transportation system, arrangements can be made to have students to board a bus in your area for transportation to and from school.

Without previous arrangements no one and I mean no one will be allowed to remove the child from the day care providers possession other than the parent. I have had brothers, grandmothers and the like attempt to pick up children. I refuse to let this happen. There have been some disgruntled people (their fault do to poor planning), but after explaining my reasoning all parents were pleased that I take that much interest in the childs welfare. Over the years I estimate that over three hundred children have been under my care. I would say that their have been approximately twenty divorces. You hear in the news quite often about parents in retaliation "stealing" the kids and leaving the state. I do not wish this to happen to children in my care. You will make arrangements prior to pickup. No Exceptions!!

When transporting children in my vehicle it is mandatory that they be buckled in, for their safety. It is the law in our state.

Backups—

You may know another provider, a relative, friend or a college student who will help you out when you need assistance. Have this person learn you routine well enough that when you have business or appointments to keep you can assure the parents that you will provide a suitable replacement. If possible have this person at your house on a number of occasions during pickup time so that the parents can become accustomed to their presence. You at times will definitely need time for yourself whether its business, pleasure or sickness. Be prepared. The parents will respect you for this as it makes complications in their life pattern when they are called and cannot bring their child to you. They also have commitments and are depending on you. After all you are a professional in your trade.

AGREEMENT—

The contract agreement will run until June 30. (Dates on your contract may be different do to your operation. December 30 of the current year is what most businesses use as the end of their fiscal year. You may want to make your year end to coincide with the end of school for the summer. Thereby you may start with a different set of children for the summer. Here you may use a brief contract thru Labor Day. (Usually the day before school starts again). Keep contracts in the same format as you could have contracts ending on twenty different dates, should they be dated to end one year from starting time. Yes you may have twenty children in your organization. Not all at the same time of course, but with before and after school children, part time, full time, and drop ins; with some Monday, Wednesday and Friday, some on Tuesday and Thursday, some twice a week, three times a week, etc. There is no end to the combinations. This is another reason that it is important to establish a schedule with each child that guarantees payment to you.

Contracts for various reasons do have to be broken. Be fair. Loss of job, illness, relocating, etc. Have a clause that requires two weeks notice prior to leaving your day care. This is were it is important that you will not be stuck. You have in your possession one weeks advance payment in addition to the Sixty Dollar Deposit. At the end you are required to return the deposit provided they are paid up to date.

Also there needs to be a clause to protect yourself in he event that you discontinue your services as a day care provider.

Circle the days and clearly write in the rates for the current contract. Keep contracts in a file box or notebook for future reference. Also have a copy made for the client so that they can refer to it prior to confronting you. The contract is your answer to most questions that may arise. Prepare it thoroughly and make notes during the year so that you can make adjustments to the contracts for the following year.

RULES and GUIDELINES

A list of rules and guidelines will constitute this chapter, therefore it will be understood that this is going on constantly and will not have to be repeated in the other chapters. The most used discipline is to have a time out. This is a few seconds sitting in a chair or on the floor away from the group. Remember just a few seconds is a long time to a small child. They do not have a recollection of time. Older children will get either a time out or write a sentence such as "I will not tell lies" twenty times or so.

Rules

Hang up coat
Put shoes in basket
Place lunch boxes on counter
No running indoors
No throwing of objects
No hugging unless you ask first
No hitting unless you ask first
Eat main course first
Eat dessert last
Clean up after lunch
Pick up toys after play
Use trash cans for trash
Wash hands after using bathroom
Put shoes on and tie them
Put on coat
Put on gloves
No name calling
No fighting
No cheating
No horseplay or roughhousing
No playing with sticks

Wait your turn
No arguments
Don't grab

The children over the age of three are capable of taking care of their belongings. If not they learn here. By the time they are five they will tie their own shoes, button or zip their coats (may need some help here) and be responsible for their lunch boxes. This saves time and work when we go on field trips.

When parents arrive to pick up their children, you may wish to inform the parent how the day went. During this time the child can put on his shoes, coat and retrieve his possessions such as lunch box, school papers, etc. The parent should not assist the children with this. Some parents will have difficulty with this at first, but will appreciate it latter. You may say in front of the parent, "Johnny can get himself ready, can't you, Johnny?"

On trips to the library and other places we work the buddy system. Each looks out for their assigned "buddy". This is a good learning system for the children, but be cautious here. THESE CHILDREN ARE YOUR RESPONSIBILITY, not that of another child.

ROUTINES

<u>Before and after school:</u>

This might be a routine day for you in providing for before and after school children.

They start arriving after 7:30 a.m. hang up their backpacks, coats and remove their shoes (Have a basket available for the shoes). Most like to play games. Here you must train them to take turns so that no one gets left out. Be very observant as to the take charge guy who manages to con the others out of a turn in some way shape or form. When this happens have this child lose a turn and if he continues or denies the infraction remove him from the group.

About fifteen minutes before the school bus arrives have the children get their shoes and coats on and get their backpacks together. If its a nice day they can now go outside and play a game such as four squares until the bus arrives.

At approximately 4:00 when the bus brings the children home, homework time is provided. Work this out with the parents as most will gladly approve. (Have a container full of pencils and a pencil sharpener on hand) You can probably enforce rules and get the children to complete their work better than the parents can at home.

After homework, on bad days back to the game playing. Good days allow for the children to romp outside. Children need to run and play to use up that excessive energy they can seem to find.

By this time the parents are picking up and before you know it your day is over.

Pre-school children:

Upon arrival lunch boxes are placed together on a counter. Coats are hung up and shoes placed in the basket. The children can now occupy themselves playing with toys for their age group. Depending on the weather a variety of activities may take place. They can be taken to the library. Maybe they will go outside and play or a video tape can be put in the VCR for them to watch.

Note: During day care hours television programs are not watched. Only selective tapes of childrens movies are used.

Then we set up for lunch. After lunch its back to play time again. Some time in mid afternoon we have a snack time. Then we go outside to play. If the weather is bad we will play inside or watch a video tape.

The children like to draw, color pictures or just use their imagination as to what is going on around them.

The younger ones like to have a couple of stories read to them. Sometimes we sing songs.

I keep a box of various types of dresses, hats scarfs, wigs, shoes, etc for the children like to dress up. (Have a wall mirror so they can see how beautiful they look)

Pictures of the children are taken in various stages of dress. As the children get older they enjoy seeing the pictures of themselves when they were "little."

BACKUP

There will be times when you cannot make appointments or commitments late in the day or on weekends. Should you call the parents to tell them that you cannot watch their child today, it may in time cost you business. Parents cannot always find someone to care for their children at the last minute and are depending on you to render them the services that you advertise. In the past fifteen years I have had on a number of occasions to be away from my place of business. Three of my daughters have had babies and I wished to be with them at the aspiring moment. My husband has had two major surgeries and I was at his side. I myself have been hospitalized several times. There have been wedding preparations, funerals and events to attend. We have visited out of town relatives. During all this I have not in the last twenty years shut down my daycare for a single day.

Early in my start up a neighbor helped me when I had a doctors appointment and etc. She visited me often and had coffee or just to make general conversation. In time she learned my routines and knew my house as well as I know it. She eventually became a primary back up provider. Also two of my daughters ventured into the child care field. They also will help me out in a bind. They became familiar with the children. When they would visit the children would ask them to help in reaching a game or to open a lunch bag. The children became very familiar with the three of them. The parents began to address them on a first name basis and were pleased to have them communicating with their children. When I go away I leave the day care children instructions that Mary is in charge and that I will keep in contact with her to see how the children are doing.

The child care phone book is with me constantly. I will call twice a day to see if there are any problems and to satisfy myself that every thing is alright. Should there be a problem with any of the children that needs parental attention the parent will be notified at the end of the day. I will make it a point to call them no matter where I am in the USA. Also when I call home, after talking with my backup, I will talk with some of the children, particularly ones that are giving the backup a difficult time. After that the provider usually has little or no trouble. The parents and children know that I am constantly overseeing operations and stay on top of situations. Always inform the parents when you will not be present.

There are a number of ways to locate a backup provider. The college in your area may have students entering into Child Psychology and are interested in studying the habits of children. They may wish to earn extra spending money at the same time further their education. There are neighbors who wish to earn an extra income but not on a full time basis. Maybe your grown children may be interested in helping mom out (for pay of course). Try the want ads in the local newspaper. The Child Support group in your area may have a listing for backkup providers. Whatever have this person to be at your home on a number of occassions to help you while you are there. They are to be shown how you do things and are to use the same methods you use when caring for the children. After this person is fmiliar and you have gained confidence in them then you can step out to the store or run a few errands. Call back by phone to see how things are going. In time you will be able to travel anywhere you like even travel in emergency or take a vacation to the beach. You will now have a backup provider.

There are days when only before and after school children are under my care. After the children go to school I may use this time to go shopping particularly around birthday times and Christmas. I will make arrangements with one of the backups to be available should I have some unforeseen delays. Should I not call the backup she knows that I am running late or tied up and she will be at my place of business when the children arrive from school.

Arrangements are made with a friend and the children are instructed that should no one be at my home when they arrive from school, they are to go to a particular neighbors house. I do not want any of my children to be stranded. That would be unconstitutional and one should be whipped with a wet noodle if that were to happen.

RECORD KEEPING

Record keeping was touched on earlier to inform you to start immediately with some form of statistics. Records are you road map and guidance as to how you are progressing. A continuous amount of documentation will be helpful as the memory is not as reliable as one might think. Records can be simple or as complicated as you wish to make them.

At the end of the year many of your clients will ask for your social security number. They may also ask you for the total of the amount paid to you for day care. This information is needed for their income tax returns. Parents are allowed a percentage deduction for child care. By keeping on going records you will not be caught trying to sift through paper work to locate the figures needed to give to the parents. What ever figure you give them there will be a few that say "that's not what I thought it was."

There are many systems in which can be used. Some prefer to do record keeping in their computers. This does nice work and gives nice print outs, but invariably the computer fails in the midst of your record keeping. We have all been in a department store, bank and the like with the statement made to us that "the computers are down."

The good old fashion notebook is as good as any system needed. (maybe better)

Have a WEEKLY record sheet such as:

	Jan 7	Jan 15	Jan 23
Jones	25.00	25.00	25.00
Canella	85.00	65.00	65.00
Mitchel	40.00	30.00	30.00
Hopkins	25.00	20.00	20.00
Klines	40.00	40.00	40.00
Boston (2)	170.00	130.00	130.00
Wilson	340.00	PD	PD
TOTAL	725.00	310.00	310.00

Insert the figures as payments are made to you.

Note that the Wilsons' like to pay a "month" at a time. Be sure you calculate this in weeks or you may be out of a couple of weeks pay and not even know it.

The Bostons' have a set of twins requiring full time services. You charge full price for each. Why should anyone get reduced rates because they have more kids. Why should you pay out of your pocket because they have more kids. No deal! Full Price.

Expenses are more difficult but records are needed and receipts available. Unless there is a CPA in the family it will be best for you to use and accountant each year for tax purposes. With your records intact they can save you quite a bit of money. In addition they will be certain that your social security requirements are taken care of. You are now a business owner and are entitled to any benefits that business owners acquire.

It is difficult, but as you grow larger in your operation a separate checking account may be useful in assisting with expense records.

Your accountant will assist you in determining what parts of your home can be used as a deduction. In the day care business you will be surprised as you need a lot more than just little office space. Practically the whole house can be used as a deduction.

With utilities a standard has not been set yet by the IRS so most accountants go with 50% of your electric, water and other utilities. You may claim depreciation for your washer, dryer, TV, VCR and you may deduct tapes that your rent or purchase for the children to watch.

You will be purchasing toilet paper in larger quantities, paper towels, and paper cups if you elect to provide them in the bathroom area.

If you purchase these materials in with your personal items keep the receipts and circle the items used for day care. Should you have a separate checking account you can pay for day care items separately. Write on the back of the receipt, what the purchase was for, record the information in you expense book and store the receipt in a box. You may never need it, but it will be there if you do. Each year start a new set of records.

For trips to the park, pool, library, store, etc. keep a record of mileages. You may deduct part of this mileage at tax time. I find the easiest method is to record the mileages to each location in a notebook and each time I make a trip to the library or where ever I simply record the date The mileage is already calculated. Then at the end of the year the number of trips X the miles gives the total mileage. Remember this mileage is round trip as you have to get back. The only flaw is if you make two stops during the same trip you will not be allowed to deduct to and from each place. Use the location the furthermost away.

Professional fees such as a lawyers (if needed) fee and the fee that your accountant charges are deductible.

After watching children for ten hours a day for five days who feels like house cleaning. Treat yourself and hire someone to clean you house every other week or more often if you prefer. After all you must keep your place of business clean and in a sanitary condition. Keep the receipts, its tax deductible.

You will at times need a back up child care provider. What you pay this provider is deductible.

Any toys or equipment such as yard equipment, swing sets, sand and sandbox, etc, purchased for you business add to the deductions.

All licenses, permits, fees and percentages of you homeowners policy are deductible. More on insurance coverage later.

The telephone in your home is not deductible, however, if you have a portable phone for outside use and a car phone or pager used for your day care, they are deductible.

Video equipment and sound intercom systems used to monitor bedrooms or play areas are deductible equipment.

Now you can see where using an accountant to work your tax papers may be very beneficial to you All you need to do is to keep records and your receipts.

Your accountant is, at most, more qualified to communicate to you what are legal deductions, how much, etc. I understand that even accountants differ on the interpretations of the IRS manuals.

TYPICAL DAY

The following is a much routine day in the care of children. It covers things that can happen after you have established guidelines for your operation.

Winter operation:

7:00 - Mrs. Jones brings Rodney, who is four years old. Rodney brings his lunch box in and sets it on the kitchen counter. He than takes of his hat, gloves and coat placing them on the hook provided for the children. He removes his shoes and places them in the plastic basket. He excitedly tells Miss Ellen that this weekend his daddy is going to take him to ride the horses. He will also remind Miss Ellen of this many times during the day. After a brief conversation with Miss Ellen, Rodney is off to the play room where he gets out the lego and starts building a car.

7:15 - Jacob who is seven now arrives and goes through the same routine. He has school books which he places with his lunch box. Jacob will get a book off the shelf and begin to read where he left off yesterday.

7:30 - 8:00 The other children arrive, Megan, Josh, Phillip, Ronald, Cagney, Lee, Liz, and Susan. Each follow the above routine and will get out games, books or drawing materials.

Note: Each child is to announce his arrival. You must always know who is under your care.

8:20 - The school age children, Megan, Josh, Cagney, Lee and Susan, will put on their shoes, coats, hats and gather their books and lunch boxes and step outside to wait on the school bus which arrives at approximately 8:30.

They may play a game of four squares or basketball. This only lasts for a few minutes, but occupies them until the arrival of the bus.

Rodney and Jacob go to a pre-school. The mothers alternate with car pooling in picking them up a 9:00 to take them to pre-school. Rodney and Jacob have dressed themselves and are ready to go when Jacobs mother arrives.

Phillip, Liz and Ronald are not yet of school age and will be here until their parents come to get them this evening. They will occupy themselves playing imaginary games, coloring or building lego.

At 12:00, Rodney and Jacob arrive from pre-school. At this time they all get their lunch boxes and sit around the table to eat their lunch and tell fantasy stories. They should have a main course (sandwich or soup) and eat this first. Than they can munch on their desert and finish their drink. This is a good routine to follow as parents are usually concerned if their child is eating. If they should consume their desert first you'll have a hard time getting them to eat their sandwich.

After lunch they put their trash in the proper container and put their lunch box which still contains the afternoon snack back on the counter.

For the next hour and twenty minutes the children can watch a film selected by Miss Ellen which is placed in the VCR. There is never any television authorized at this day care. Only selected video tapes. TV has commercials on upcoming programs which are not suitable for small children to see and in changing channels one never know what is going to jump from the screen. TV programs are not needed in a well planned day care center.

It is now 2:30 and if the day is nice the children can have their snack outside prior to playing. These children are very young, so they should be monitored constantly.

A swing set, with swings only, is probably the most utilized outside piece of equipment. A play house would be an asset. Otherwise children can amuse themselves with imaginary fantasies. We cannot play with sticks or throw anything other than a ball which cannot hurt anyone. Keen discretion must be used here to prevent a child from getting hurt. The children should not wrestle or get involve in horseplay.

At 4:00, Megan, Josh, Cagney, Lee and Susan arrive from school by way of bus. They may have their snack and than spend the next hour working on any homework assignment they may have. (Provide an area for them to work) Usually you have worked this out with the parents. Believe me the parents will appreciate this as they themselves have a lot to do after arriving at home and getting the children to do their home work or helping them is difficult. Also this keeps the children occupied near the end of the day. Should they not have homework than they can utilize outside play. In time you will be familiar with the school teachers routine and will know what the students' responsibilities are.

At 4:15 Jacobs' mom picks him up and tells you that Wednesday her sister will bring Jacob and pick him up as she has a meeting to attend (remember, no one is to pick up a child without previous authorization). While you are talking with Jacobs' mom, Jacob is putting on his shoes, coat, hat and gathering together his drawings and lunch box.

As Jacob and his mom exit in comes Lizs' father. He tells you that Liz will be here the remainder of the week with the exception of Friday. At this time remind the father to see that a check is left on Thursday as you will not see them Friday. If the parent does not come in the house when they bring their children and the child is small instruct the parent to place the check in the childs' lunch box.

At five o'clock Cagneys' mom pulls in the driveway. She is in a hurry and blows the horn for Cagney. You observe this and on the next day that Cagney comes to your daycare, take the mother aside and explain to her that your are in agreement with the neighbors that they will not be disturbed by hornblowing or other unusual noises. Also explain that a child is not to leave your property without first coming to you; letting you know that they are leaving and with who. Nip these type problems in the bud to prevent them from continuing.

At 5:10 when Rodneys mom comes he immediatly runs to her and starts hitting her. Then he falls on the floor and kicks his feet. This kid had been as good as gold all day, but now he all of a sudden has this extra energy that he feels he must burn off. Tell the parent that this is not acceptable behavior in your house and that tomorrow when Rodney comes he will do a time out. This is a very effective method. Rodney may not want to come tomorrow, knowing the consequence. But, mom works with you. She brings Rodney and you immediately have him take a time out. Then have him explain to you why he is taking a time out. (I don't know is not a reason). This should be done before he is allowed to go play.

When Phillips father picks him up, Phillip puts on his shoes, grabs his lunch box and hurries out to the car. His dad is taking him to see a friend. After hours you observe that Phillip forgot his coat. Whoops! Tomorrow morning a time out for Phillip. He will learn to take care of his responsibilities.

Megan and Joshs' mothers come in and sit at the table to discuss upcoming shool events, extra curricular activities or dance lessons that the children are getting involve in. (You may wish to have a pot of coffee available and offer them a cup). You in time will be very involved in the activities of the children. Learn the instructors names, phone numbers and any information pertaining to the activities that you may pass on to other parents.

As you are talking to the parents Lees' mom calls and says that she will be about fifteen minutes late. You give her the OK as you do not have another commitment. This is to remind you to remind all parents that if they are going to be late it is important that they call you. Reason being your work day ends at 5:30 and you schedule appointments for yourself after this time. Have the parent be prepared to get someone else to pick up in the event they are going to be late or have a disignated place that you can drop off their child on your way out. My children were involved in after school sports so I took the daycare children that were left with me to the event. Arrangements were made with the parents in advance to pick up at the ball field or where ever. The kids loved the change of pace.

At 5:30 Ronalds mother and Susans' father arrive to get their children. You remind them both that Wednesday is a half day at school and ask them if they want the children to come to your house. This is important so that you will know how to schedule your activites for Wednesday. They will more than likely say "yes", but it is very important to have a clear understanding.

At 5:40 Lees' mother arrives an apologies for being late. A last minute project came up at work. This is a good time to tell here that it was not a problem today, but it could have been should you have had a commitment of your own. Then explain to her about someone else being authorized to pick up the child or having a designated place that you can take him.

41

After all have gone, take a look around to make sure you don't have any stowaways. Its always possible one could have laid on a couch or bed and went to sleep. Don't immediatly leave the house without checking. Believe me it can happen, with confusion and a late parent not calling. Always Check.

This is how most days will go. Of course there will be many things that differ from day to day pending the weather, school closings, etc.

Note: Five of these children were occupied with school for seven and one half hours. Two of the children were involved in pre-school for three hours. Therefore most of you day was tending to three young children. This leaves you a lot of time to take care of phone calling, bill paying, bookkeeping, if you so desire.

Five before and after children 200.00

Two pre-schoolers you keep three days a week 100.00

Three full time children 285.00

Wednesday half day at school (extra hours) 70.00
TOTAL 655.00

How many people can earn this figure and stay at home all week? Have a helper and if you have the space you can far exceed these earnings

Summer operation:

OK school is out which means you will have the before and after children all day and most likely five days a week. You may also acquire the older brothers or sisters of the pre-schoolers.

0700 - Mrs. Jones brings four year old Rodney and also Rodneys older sister, Janet, who previously was in school all day. This time of year there is no need for coats, hats and gloves so added space for this is not needed. They will put their lunch boxes on the kitchen counter, put their shoes in the basket and venture to the play area.

0715 - Jacob who was a before and after school child will now be full time for the summer arrives. He goes through the routine with his personal belongings and than occupies himself with a new puzzle.

0730 - 0800 The other children arrive, Megan, Josh, Phillip, Ronald, Cagney, Lee, Liz, and Susan. Each follow the above routine and will get out games, books or drawing materials. Megan, Josh, Cagney, Lee, and Susan are now full timers for the summer.

Again each child will announce their arrival to you. Should a child not arrive it is in the best interest to contact the parent to find out where the break in communication happened.

The pre-schoolers Rodney and Jacob are also full time for the summer. You now have eleven full time children for the summer. Think about it. At the suggested rates that is eleven times ninety-five dollars or One Thousand Forty Five dollars a week. This weekly for the summer could build a nice nest egg near Thirteen Thousand Dollars for three months work. More than a lot of people make in a year. With this many children it is suggested, of course, that you obtain additional help It could be a college student studying child psychology or a housewife seeking to supplement the family income.

OK all the children have arrived to begin the day. They will now be able to utilize the outside yard much more if the weather is agreeable. When outside they play four squares, soccer, softball (with a plastic bat and ball), swing, play in the sand box (be prepared to keep the neighborhood cats out), dodge ball or a number of play ground games. It is important to oversee the playtime and to hold down any rowdiness.

They will play until 10:00 o'clock which is snack time. They may utilize the nice weather and have their snack on the back porch or at the picnic table. Provide a trash container for the children to place trash and containers in. When finished with their lunch they will place the lunch boxes on the kitchen counter.

Maybe now we will go to the recreation center to play at the play ground or to the library to get some new books. We may take in a matinee at the movies. We may eat lunch at the playground or return home.

After lunch we may go to the swimming pool. Remember all parents have agreed in the beginning that this is a part of your summer program and have paid a membership for the children. After you have had the children for a while and have enforced the rules on a regular basis the children will be little or no trouble at the pool. You will probably be able to control your group better than some of the parents can handle their own children. Of course you will have your helper take care of the smaller children in the wading pool, while you have the older ones at the main pool. Most will learn to swim, jump off the diving board and handle themselves in deep water. Its amazing what children can do when exposed to an activity.

We may stay at the pool all afternoon having made arrangements with the parents to pickup their children from the pool.

If it is unusually hot we will return home about three o'clock and have our afternoon snack. We can watch a video, play games, read, or color. We are now tired and winding down. The parents are coming in to pick up their children. A few will stay around and discuss the childrens activities, maybe even have a cup of coffee should you elect to offer some. Before you know it the day is gone.

It is wise to prepare yourself to handle activities smoothly and without confusion or lack of equipment. I handle the pool operations in this manner. I purchased a dozen duffel bags and put a tag on each bag bearing a childs name and a picture in a laminated card. The child has a swim suit, towel and any other swimming items that they may need. We put on our swim suits prior to leaving home and take our duffel bags with us. When we return home we remove our swim suits and place them in a laundry basket along with our towels. Sometime this evening I will place the suits and towels in the washing machine. In the morning each child will go through the clean clothes basket and pick out their swim suit and towel. They will then put the items in their duffel bag and be ready for out next trip. The duffel bags are mine and are used every summer.

BARTERING

Since taking up a day care operation, people in a variety of occupations have used my services. A few of these occupations have been a department store manager, doctors, lawyers, a social services director, a windshield glass replacement owner, refrigeration mechanics, a real estate developer, a computer specialist, a radio announcer, a veterinarian, nurses, restaurant owners, an architect, a baker, a pharmacist, a psychologist, professors, a airline pilot, winery staff personal, seamstresses, a Division of Motor Vehicle supervisor, school teachers, a minister, landscapers, painters, musicians and a music teacher and shop operator.

Working with these people have provided great opportunities in learning and trade off providing a savings to my family. My very first client was a veterinarian. After a few years we developed a friend ship. When our pet dog of sixteen years passed on, the vet had a puppy that was found on the street. The puppy would have been put to sleep had the vet not found a home for it. She offered me the puppy with and agreement that she would take care of all veterinarian bills for the life of the dog. This was an offer I could not refuse. My children had a new pet for the next ten years and we never had a veterinarian bill during this time.

Another opportunity came when our second daughter was to be married. A seamstress for whose child I was taking care of was very excited for my daughter and altered all the bridesmaids dresses from the first wedding by changing the lace and hems. Instead of accepting payment she took it out in child care.

Another seamstress made curtains for my daughters house for the cost of the material. Labor was taken out in child care.

We had blueprints drawn up for us by a architect to design a new home that we would like to build. Again this was taken out in child care.

Through the airline pilot we were able to obtain tickets round trip from Virginia to Florida for a very low rate. There was no trade off here, just having the right connection.

There have been pharmacists that have given us advice about various prescriptions and how taken with other medicines may affect our health. Also they armed me with important questions to seek from my personal doctor.

One restaurant owner who had connections with the Washington Redskin organization was able to get us tickets to see the Redskins play in Washington D.C.

Also through restaurant owners we were able to purchase meats and other products at lower prices than the consumer.

At Christmas time, a store manager, gave us a discount on all merchandise that we purchased through his place of business.

We had the windshields on our van a pickup truck repaired by a windshield repairer who informed us that the insurance company would waiver our deductible to have this done. To repair the chips to the insurance companies is apparently cheaper than replacing a windshield.

A computer specialist advised me on what computer to purchase for my husband as a gift and it was ordered from a computer discount store. He also later installed a modem card in the computer as a surprise for my husband. This was performed for the cost of the card and modem.

Nurses with many years of experience advised both me and my husband on selected surgeons to perform major operations on the two of us.

When I lost my billfold including my drivers license the Department of Motor Vehicle supervisor told me how to replace it. She said, "You need to have your birth certificate or know somebody." I had my drivers license replaced that afternoon.

School teachers keep me informed as to upcoming school events and outside programs that would be offered. A number of my children thus are involved in gymnastics, ballet and a variety of activities.

Musicians and tutorers came to my place of business to train and teach children in music and school academics. This was a big savings to the parents in the way of transportation and being able to stay on the job.

Unfortunately I never had an automobile mechanic or an accountant, both which I could have gained a great deal of information.

The baker made cakes, deserts and prepared foods for a daughters baby shower.

Personally knowing these people made these opportunities convenient.

So, you see when you are involved with children the opportunity exists for one to meet many interesting people, involved in many different professions. Most all of the above were offered to me as I did not make any advance deals. The opportunities came up in casual conversation after the clients were known for a while. Personally knowing these people made it possible for me to make changes in designs and seek what was available at any time.

INSURANCE

Yes there is a need to carry a liability insurance for protection of the business. There is always the possibility of an accident of some sort and it is best to be prepared. A child may be seriously hurt in some strange manner or a parent can fall off your doorstep. Wonders never cease.

Check with your homeowners insurance company to see what provisions your policy covers. Some will cover day care by charging an additional fee and placing a rider onto your policy. Some homeowners insurance companies will not insure a business. There are a number of companies who will insure your business, however, with most, the rates are extremely high. Check with several companies to find rates suitable for you.

Most all parents (with children under my care) carry a hospitalization plan and the children who may have injuries are covered. The plan that you are looking for is to cover serious accidents which are seldom, if any, ever happen but one needs to be prepared.

Insuranace companies charge by the number of children that are under you care. Rates are also determined by conditions such as do you have a pool in your back yard? Or, do you have a dog for a pet and is it isolated from the children by being kept in a separate yard?

The insurance companies will send you a questionnaire to complete and as you complete the form you will see at that time what your rates will be.

Insurance will most likely be the highest expense one encounters in the daycare business so use discretion as to what company you will use and what you needs may be.

Be certain to check with the Insurance Commissioner to be certain that this company is authorized to do business in your state.

QUESTIONS & ANSWERS

Many incidents or questions arise that happen when caring for children that would be difficult to cover in paragraph form. I find the best way to do this is with questions and answers, thereby we can focus on isolated happenings.

Many day care providers get put into difficult situations, simply, because they are confronted with a question or incident in which they do not know how to respond. The best solution to operating a business is to know your business so that you will answer problem questions with ease. In knowing what to say the less assertive you will need to be.

1. What if a prospective client seems to be sincere, needs day care but cannot afford to put down a deposit or pay a week in advance?

    You can suggest that along with each of the first few weeks fee that they pay an extra ten dollars until the deposit or a weeks advance is covered. It is important that you get that deposit. It may save you from losing out on a weeks work when this client no longer needs your services.

2. What should I do when a friend asks me to watch her children?

    For a few hours or even a day I would not charge a friend. However do not let it become a habit. You are a very busy person and cannot afford to take too much time away from your children.

3. Should I get involved with the schools?

    Yes, by all means, even join the PTA. This is one of your very best sources of advertising and it gives you access to activities in which to involve your children. Taking preschoolers to plays, pizza parties, Halloween parties, etc, gives the pre-school children an idea what goes on at the school. This teaches them how to conduct themselves. The parents will be very happy that you participate and will most likely be a client of yours for a long time.

4. What if a child brings his favorite teddy bear with him?

    The child may bring a toy if they are willing to share it with others. If they are not willing to do this than the toy will be put away until they leave. Some day care providers say absolutely no toys. Your call.

5. Do I need to give anyone my social security number?

    Yes. The parents may deduct a portion of the costs of child care on their taxes and may need either your social security number or a tax identification number, whichever you prefer they use.

6. Why should I not keep children after 5:30?

    Establish a working day and make it consistent. You also have a life to attend to, commitments, and need time to yourself. To push yourself into excessive work may cause you to become burned out, stressed and lose interest in what you are doing.

7. Some day care center prepare meals and charge more. Why should I not do this?

    Preparing meals is very time consuming in that you must first grocery shop in addition to your own household shopping, attempt to get something daily that everyone likes, prepare it, serve it and clean up. OK if you like restaurant work. Let the parents pack the lunches, that way they can pack what the child likes. Well, if the child complains its not your fault!

8. What should I do if a child has several bruises and seems withdrawn?

    Contact the social services department in your area. They will handle the case very confidentially. You owe it to the child.

9. What should I do if a child gets hurt?

    Perform the necessary first aid. If the injury is severe call 911 or the emergency number for your area. Notify the parents immediately. Parents must be told of all incidents regardless of how small the incident may be. The parent will than use judgement on how to follow up. They must also know that they can trust you completely. Better they hear what happened from you than from the child after they get home. Regardless as to what the child tells them they will already have your view of the happening. Be totally honest with the parents.

10. What if a parent tells me "I am short on cash, could I pay you next week?"

    If this parent is a long time client and has been very reliable in the past give the ok. However if this has become a problem and you practically have to beg for your payment than tell the parent that you cannot operate this way. Give them notice that you will no longer perform services for them after they locate another child care provider. Tell them that you will attempt to find a provider for them. There are special services in the area for parents who cannot afford to pay for day care. Two weeks is plenty of notice.

11. Should I attend any school or community functions?

    Yes as many as you feel comfortable in attending. There are swim meets, pool parties, recreation center activities. Most of these are free or require a very small fee. Attending these functions help you to become know in the community along with occupying part of the day and provides a variety of things for the children to do.

12. How do I handle a situation where a parent is continually late for pick up?

    Attempt to ward this of the second time that it happens. Tell the parent that you do not work beyond 5:30 and would appreciate it if they would pick up by that time. Inform them that, when possible you schedule your appointments after 5:30 when the children have left. Remind them of the agreement in the beginning. If they cannot be at your place of business by the appointed time than maybe they should seek day care from someone who will meet their needs. You may if you desire keep children after the scheduled time provided the parent calls and says that they are running late.

If you do not have anything planned than you can accommodate them, but if you have a commitment they will have to pick up or you can take the child to a designated drop off spot. It is very important that the parent make the phone call to you to inform you of their situation. This gives you opportunity to make arrangements if necessary.

13. The mother usually pays me on Friday, but when the father picks up I do not get my check until next week.

Inform both parents of the need to make timely payments. The child either brings a lunch or snack every day that he is under your care. A check can be placed in his lunch box at the time that the meal is packed.

14. What if I see a child with head lice?

Inform the childs parent and inform the other parents that one of the children has contacted head lice and is being treated. Some parents may become alarmed. Tell them that this is quite common among children and is easily corrected.

15. A parent does not want their child to attend a movie with the other children, reason unknown.

Remember the interview, remember the contract? What has suddenly steered the parent? Tell the parent again that you only take children to see PG rated movies and would not want the child to feel left out. Should the parent insist than tell the parent that they will have to provide care by someone else during the time that you are having an outing with the children.

16. When the children check out books from the library who is responsible to see that the books are returned?

    I would make it my responsibility as I plan to make use of the facility for a long time to come. I do not need the reputation of a person who brings in a group of irresponsible kids.

17. I only have one bathroom in my home. What are good bathroom rules?

    Provide small dispenser drinking cups and paper towels. Teach boys to lift the seat when using the toilet. One child at a time. Others wait outside the door until the user is finished with the bathroom. Do not linger when occupying bathroom.(Have a trash can. Paper towels won't flush)

18. What if an after school child does not get off the bus when it arrives?

    Contact the parent immediately. More than likely the parent forgot to inform you that the child would not be there today. If that was not the case the parent can start a immediate investigation to find out what went wrong.

19. I hear some of the children that I keep has caused a disruption on the school bus. Should I intervene?

    Definitely. The conduct of the children that you care for says a lot about your reputation. You need to work with the bus driver as you will also need the driver to work with you. Both of you are concerned for the childrens safety.

20. A child tells the parent that I am too strict.

Talk this over with the parent to see what their feelings are on the allegation. Make certain that truthful statements were made. If the complaint is within the manner in which you use discipline than you will need to inform the parent this is the way you run your operation. If they feel this is not within their desires they should look for another provider.

21. A child is here on Tuesdays and Thursdays. This Tuesday the child does not come. Later Tuesday afternoon the parent calls to ask me if they could bring the child Wednesday to make up the day missed.

You will take the child only if you have a vacancy for that day and the parent will be responsible for the additional payment for that day. (at your daily rate) Once you have established a schedule stick to it unless it needs to be changed on a permanent basis.

22. My own children are in school and some activities begin prior to the 5:30 pick up. What should I do?

All activities are scheduled ahead of time. Work this out with the parents that they can pick up their children at the ball field, at the swimming pool or were ever the activity may be. You will find that the children enjoy going to such activities for a change of pace. Take their belongings with them and a blanket for them to sit on.

23. Is it OK for a parent to stop in front of the house and blow the horn for the child to come out?

Tell the parent that you have made an agreement with the neighbors that there would be no unusual noises resulting from your day care operation. If the parents need to be in a hurry they can call you before they leave the office and you can have the child ready to go when they arrive.

24. I find a child missing from the yard and one of the children tell me, "Joeys dad came and got him."

Call Joeys house to verify this and tell the parents that you need to be informed that a child is being picked up. This is for the safety of the child, to prevent creating confusion and so that you will have the opportunity to tell the parents any needed information.

25. Mr. Jones has become ill and cannot work. The Jones tell me that they cannot afford to give me a two weeks notice. Should I keep their deposit?

No. Every family at one time or another has a crisis and needs the help of someone. You can be flexible with your guidelines at such a time.

26. Is it possible that I may ever have to attend a court session?

There are custody battles when parents divorce and it is very possible that the parent dealing with you may give the lawyer your name as their child care provider. They may want you for a character reference for the parent.

27. A new child I find is not yet potty trained. Do I tell the parent not to bring him:

Children in your age group usually are potty trained, however there are exceptions. Tell the parent that you will work with the child in attempt to train him. After a period of time if you do not succeed than you can tell the parent that you do not have time to continue changing the child and they can bring him back when he is trained. (Usually in a short time the child will be trained. Its amazing what day care providers can do that parents can't.)

28. A child was disruptive at the library today. What is the best method to resolve what happened?

When arriving back on your grounds talk with the child about what was not appropriate at the library than have the child either take a time out or write twenty five times "I must behave at the library."

29. Can I have pets in my home during day care?

If you have a cat and the cat is gentle it is appealing to let the cat roam. Most children love cats and will want to cuddle it or play with it. Be cautious of those who may decide to torment it. Discipline is in order for any cruelty to the animal. Dogs may be a different story. Most insurance companies require that a dong be kept in a separate yard away from the children. Be alert for children who may have allergies that act up if they are in the vicinity of domestic animals. In this case the pets must be separated from the children.

30. A parent is sometimes asked at work to stay a little longer. This means they will be late getting to my place.

Again a phone call is needed to inquire as to your desires. You may accommodate the parents needs or they may need to have a backup to pick up their child. This needs to be worked out with the parents in the beginning as last minute situations can be difficult on everyone.

31. Parents sometimes forget their checkbook. I would like to have my money.

    Its Friday and its payday. Ask the parent to bring the check to you. If necessary tell them that you will pick it up. Then ask them in the future to pay you on Thursday, a day ahead of time. Should they forget this allows time for a reminder to pay you Friday.

32. Would I benefit from seminars and/or workshops?

    By all means. There will be many seminars and workshops on day care operations. There will be meetings with guest speakers on insurance plans, record keeping, discipline and other aspects related to day care. One benefits from all the information that is available.

33. What kinds of notes and documentations should I keep, if any?

    It is not really necessary to keep documentations however one could keep a page for unusual situations to serve as a backup reminder should there be a difference of opinion later. Such as a child was disruptive on the school bus for a couple of days. Months later the situation comes up again and the parent swears that their child did not have a previous incident. Your documentation as to the incident, date, time and those involved may have the parent suddenly regain their memory.

34. I am talking with a parent and a child is listening to our conversation.

    Send the child to another area to play until you have finished your conversation and the parent has left. Than tell the child that they are not to stand around and listen to you talking with other people when they are supposed to be elsewhere. Children understand very well what you are saying. Some may be a little stubborn, but they understand. Communication is the most important tool you have with both the parents and the children. They are not mind readers and will many times not know what to do until you tell them. So speak up and let your desires be known.

35. A child has had a good day but the moment his parent steps into the house the child acts silly and starts hitting the parent.

Its strange how the sight of a parent can cause a childs adrenaline to start flowing. Your recourse is to tell the parent that you do not allow the child to act in such a manner and that you will take care of it tomorrow. Tomorrow when the child arrives he is reminded of the way that he acted when his mom came yesterday and is told of your disapproval. Then the child will do a time out. Surprisingly the children learn on short order how to behave. Have this child occupied when the parent comes such as putting on their shoes, coat, hat, etc.

36. A child has left his backpack at school with his homework in it.

Remind him that he is responsioble for his belongings and his school work as well. Should it happen again than he is to do a time out or write twenty five times. "I must remember to bring my homework from school." The child now has to answer to you, his parents and to the teacher when the home work is not completed.

37. A child is in a hurry to play with the other children. He throws his coat on the floor and runs to play.

    Whoops! Time out for not hanging up the coat and for running in the house.

38. A child who is usually brought to the house at 9:00 a.m. has not arrived. It is now 10:00 and we are ready to go to a special play.

    You normally have a schedule to keep and cannot stay around waiting for others. A phone call would have been helpfull but it was not received. Continue with your plans. Do not hold up the activities of the children because of one individual.

39. Does my homeowners insurance cover an injury?

    There is a good chance that it will not cover a injury that is related to a home operated business. It is best to contact the insurance company and find out what their policy is on this. They may issue you a rider, a complete policy or you may have to take this type of insurance out with another company.

40. My neighbor has two children who know my daycare kids from school. They want to come over and play with them.

    There are a number of risk factors here. First are you at your quota? Normally children who are not under your services are not considered as part of your quota. Check the regulations in your county. Should there be an injury who is responsible? You. Keep control over this. Allow it sometimes but not every day. Simply tell the children that you are very busy and they may come at another time.

41. One of my daycare children would like to go home with my neighbors child.

    If the parent tells you of this, than you have no problem with it. You are being paid anyway.

42. Kids have their curiosity and I find one who has said to another, "You show me yours and I'll show you mine."

    Tell the children that this is not the kind of play allowed at your house. Than tell the parents about it so that they may act accordingly. Tell the parents not to be alarmed for most all children come to this at sometime in their lives. Being scolded is not the answer, just a good talk with the child and it more than likely will not happen again.

43. A parent drops off his child and leaves. I find the child standing outside.

    Have a talk with the parent. Tell them that they must make sure that you are available. One never knows when you may have an emergency and leave home in a hurry. This may not give you time to contact all parents. It is the parents responsibility to see that their children are in safe hands.

44. The children have singled out a child and will not allow her to play with them.

    Find out why the children feel this way and who suggested that the child cannot play. Usually there is a leader or controlling child. You need to find how this started and see to it that it does not continue. Let it be known to the children that eveyone is included in playtime. Then form an activity supervised by you that all the children will participate in.

45. A child has hurt another child. The parent says that, "My child would not do that."

    If you have trained your children there is little chance of this happening. Should it be intentional, it must be dealt with. You have already established with the children what happened so you must tell the parent that their child did hurt the other child. Tell the parent that you have disciplined the child and that they may wish to have a talk with him.

46. A child would rather wet his pants than stop playing to go to the bathroom.

    This is almost the same as a child who needs potty training. The exception is that this child has already been trained and knows what he has done. This child needs a periodic reminder to use the bathroom. After a period of time he will become accustomed to this.

47. A parent calls and says, "I won't be bringing Joey to your house anymore."

    First find out the reason for this and than remind the parent that a two week notice is required. Should the parent stand by their statement you have the security deposit as well as a weeks advanced payment in your possession.

48. This same parent calls in about two weeks and would like to come back to your daycare.

    Business is business. They may start a new contract and pay a new deposit provided that you have a space available for them.

49. I have a handicapped child. How should I treat them?

     The handicapped child should be treated the same as the other children with no favoritism shown because of the handicap. The child wants to feel as normal as possible and will learn to deal with his handicap in his own way.

50. Some of my children may need tutoring or have music lessons to attend. Should I be involved in any way?

     You could arrange to have the tutor hold sessions in your home. This would save the parents the trouble of pick up and delivery. They are certainly going to appreciate this. Remember word of mouth is your biggest asset.

51. Any ideas about birthdays, Christmas, Halloween, etc?

     Hold a small party recognizing a childs birthday. Also a Halloween party and be prepared for the little goblins coming to your house on Halloween night. I make it a practice to give each child a small gift and a two dollar bill for Christmas.

52. What about religion?

     It is not a good idea to discuss religion as different families are of different denominations and some are very particular as to what their children are exposed to in the way of religion.

53. Should it be alright for the older children to watch TV?

     I do not utilize the TV with the exception of showing selected tapes. There is no need for television and it should not be used as a means to occupy time.

54. I cannot get back home in time for the arrival of my children and cannot possibly contact the parents?

    A plan has previously been made with the children to go to a certain neighbors house in the event I am not available. Prior arrangements will be made with that neighbor before I leave home.

55. A parent normally picks his child up at 4:00. Today I am fifteen minutes late getting home from the pool with the kids. The parent is arrogant and blasts me for having him wait. How should I handle this situation?

    Tell the parent how you feel. (Calmly of course.) To rush would have put the safety of the children in jeopardy. I am sure that this very parent does not have a perfect track record when it comes to being on time. Tell the parent you are sorry that you were late and do not feel that his being obnoxious is necessary. You do not abuse other people and you do not expect to be treated as such.

56. Children tell their parents stories and the parents believe them.

    Converse with the parents on a daily basis. Inform them of their childs day both on the good side as well as any problems that have occurred. After time if you are consistently honest you will have built trust in the parents. You have told the parents from the original interview, therefore they already perceive how you conduct your business. Confront the child in the parents presence. Allow the child to back down graciously. The parent will get the message.

57. A clients check is returned from the bank marked "insufficient funds."

Remind the parent that you will take cash as the bank charges you for returned checks, in addition you have to make adjustments to your bank account.

58. What organizations can help day care providers and how?

In your area there is a children's support group. They charge a very small fee for you to be a member of their organization. Their mission is to see that children are well taken care of. They will pay you a visit and provide recommendations. They have your name listed and when people in you area request daycare they may refer these prospects to you. The support group provides group meetings on subjects helpful to providers on discipline, operations, insurance, safety, health, bookkeeping, etc.

Social Services in your area will inform you how to obtain a food plan should you desire to make lunches for the children. They may provide assistance to persons who cannot afford to pay for day care.

59. What ways are there to find children for day care

The most used of course is word of mouth. You being professional and concerned for the childrens well being will definitely bring many clients in this manner. Other methods include the use of business cards when you are at functions, other providers will refer you to persons they cannot accept, support groups are consistently referring their members to clients. Also advertising in the community newspaper will bring calls.

60. How can I do day care for someone who cannot afford it?

    Have them contact Social Services. They will need to fill out proper forms and pending their situation Social Services may see that they get the necessary funds. In this manner you would be guaranteed payment. Social Services may ask that you provide them with an on going record of the time the child or children are under your care.

61. A parent says, "My mother is visiting and she will watch my kids next week".

    This is fine, however your client is under contract and will pay you for the week the child is not under your care.

62. A child does not arrive by bus in the evening. Should I be concerned?

    If you have not been notified by the parent that the child was not coming to your day care today by all means find out where the child is. Start with a call to the parents. This may settle the question. Should it not than the parents will follow up with the necessary tracing. You may, if you desire to call numbers that you are familiar with and should you find the location of the child, immediately contact the parents. There are many reasons while a child may not be on the bus and it will probably happen to you on occasion.

63. One of my day care children has not been trained. He is older than some that are. What recourse do I have?

    It does not take long in most cases to train a child. Talk with the parent about this. Was it not mentioned during the interview? You may want to work on training the child yourself. Somewhere, for some reason the parents did not see the need to do this or did not know how to. Your continuous contact with children will teach you a lot that parents do not learn. In a short time you will feel like a pro.

64. A parent does not bring a child one morning and I was not notified that they were not coming. Should I contact the parent?

Yes, there could have been a breakdown in communications with the child, or with someone else who was to bring the child to your home. Find out to be certain that the child is safe.

65. A child falls and hurts himself prior to the arrival of the school bus. By the time the bus arrives he is OK. Should I be of further concern?

The parent of the child should be notified as well as the school nurse. The school than can inform the teacher to monitor the childs actions and report unusual movements that may occur.

66. Mike tells me that Johnathan took a toy away from him. Johnathan says not so. Who do I believe?

Talk with both children. Have them each explain what happened. (With no interruptions) You can usually determine from their story and observing their actions what prevailed. If you feel that you have settled the incident than allow the first child to continue playing with the toy for a time period. Than allow the other child to have a turn. Should you not be sure than divert the children into playing something else and put the toy away.

67. A child has fallen off the swing and bumped his head. After a brief crying spell he appears to be OK. Should I bother to tell the parent?

    Definitely, make it a point to. Inform the parent what has happened and tell them that you will keep observation as to the childs actions. Should you see the child become disoriented contact the parent again so that they may seek medical attention.

68. A mother and father are having problems and when talking to me they have a tenancy to bad mouth the spouse. Do I need to listen to this?

    It does not hurt to listen as the parent feels a need to talk to someone, however do not take sides. You are not a counselor nor do you know what is really going on.

69. A lot of rules have been listed. Are they all really necessary?

    Yes, then some. The rules are what makes your day care a success. Parents cannot believe that a group of children can play without constant disruption and know what to do in the way of caring for themselves. Children are quite intelligent and most like being independent.

70. Why do I need to be assertive and stick so closely to the guidelines mentioned in this book?

    Well! they come from over twenty five years of experience and have helped me to become quite successful in the day care business. Assertiveness is not being pushy. It is knowing your business and having the answers when situations arise. Than you will feel at ease in presenting the facts to a parent.

71. I am talking to a parent or on the phone when one of the children constantly attempts to get my attention. Should I excuse myself from the person that I am talking to?

I would to find out what the child needs. If it is not overly important tell the child to go play and you talk with him latter. After your phone conversation call the child back and help the child to determine when you can be interrupted, such as in an emergency. Help the child to determine what is an emergency.

72. When something goes wrong its easier to make up an excuse than to explain the circumstances. Is this good practice?

No, its not. Again be totally honest with your parents. There will be times when matters are difficult for the parents to accept but they must learn that you are very sincere in what you are doing and in time you will earn their respect.

73. One of the parents informs you that they do not care for the back up provider. Do I take up for my assistant because I know her better than the parent?

Ask the parent what it is that concerns them. Explain the providers background. You have of course had a criminal background check on the back up provider and a TB screen test. Unless the parent has truthful adverse information on the backup provider you stick with the provider. Thank the parent for their concerns and inform them that you will continue to use this person.

74. A child who has not been a problem suddenly begins to wet his pants. What is the reason for this?

Usually there is a problem in the family circle at home. Tell the parent of the childs sudden change and let them work on it in their own manner. Some will ask for advice. Then knowing the parent you will need to use discretion on explaining your thoughts.

75. A new parent claims that the last day care provider was a bummer. What may I have learned from this?

You will learn the parents concerns. Perhaps you know the previous provider. You will use this information to determine if you welcome this parent into your day care operation.

76. When I ask a child a question and she refuses to answer, what options do I have?

You apparently asked the child, do to a circumstance. Refusing to answer usually means the child does not want to for they feel there will be a consequence. Have the child do a time out until they are ready to talk about what is going on. Ask the child periodically if they would like to tell you now.

77. There is one parent who verbally abuses me. How do I stop this?

I would jump on this one at the very beginning. Unless the parent can control their emotions and use better manners than tell them that you will no longer do day care for them. Give them a two week notice. This is in all fairness for them to find someone else. If they are annoyed or disturbed about this they may leave immediately.

78. A mother mentions one day how wonderful her child is. Here at my home the child fibs constantly. Do I tell her this?

Again this is something that you should have brought up in the beginning, than it would not have gotten to this. Each day inform the parent what took place during the day. This gives the parent opportunity to address any given situation. Remember the child sees more of you and is in contact more with you possibly more than they are with their parents.

79. A mother complains that her son won't get dressed in the morning and that she has difficulty leaving the house in time to bring the child and than get to work on time.

Tell her to bring the child as he is. Yes, in his pajamas. If she wishes she may bring along his clothes. Once should be enough to have the child scrambling to get dressed in the mornings.

80. Every now and than a parent does not understand what I am going through during the day and makes me very angry. Should I stand my ground and tell this rude person off?

Again constant communication is needed to keep the parents informed. There should be no long standing surprises. When the child has had a good day tell the parents this. When the child has not had a good day discuss it with the parent.

"Ms. Ellen"

SUMMARY

Mentioned in the beginning were reasons in which you may wish to take up day care. Yes, you may wish to work with children or may prefer to stay at home and work rather than going out into the hustle and bustle of the working force. What ever the reasons you can be sure that you are in it for the money. Tell me that you would watch children for no payment.. I don't think so. So, using the information you have just covered will keep dollars from slipping through your fingers. You work for it and you deserve it.

Remember the safety and well being of the children are your first concern. Be on the alert for unsafe conditions and have these corrected or removed. Learn the actions of children, which will indicate many things. Look for signs of abuse.

You are literally raising the children under your care. Some will be with you up to nine hours a day. At most their parents get three hours with them which includes preparing dinner, washing clothes, preparing bath water, etc. What these children learn from you sets a pattern in their life. Make their learning positive, enjoyable and meaningful.

Other than telling a parent the good things that their child did, make all other conversations one on one with the parent. You and the parent may be pondering a decision on handling situations. If overheard by the child, he may think the two of you are having an argument. The child does not need to have things that he doesn't understand to upset or scare him.

You are in business to perform a service You are not a servant. The operation is yours, your decisions. Set up a routine that will apply to your operation. Explain from the beginning to each perspective parent. They then have to decide as to whether they wish to use your services.

Start with a plan. Make a list of interview items to cover, i.e., your responsibilities, the parents responsibilities and the childs responsibilities. Take items from the contract for review and discuss with the parents. State your intentions or course of action in normal conversation with the parent. Do not sound demanding, pushy or macho.

In the beginning you will probably acquire about two children and go from there. It won't take long before you will have a waiting list. Do not take on more than you are comfortable with. You will find later as you progress that you can handle a few more and how to fill in the gaps.

In the beginning I didn't think to take pictures, but in the last ten years I have taken a picture of each child. Write their name, age and date on the back. Post the picture on a large bulletin board and watch your family grow. The kids enjoy having their picture "on the wall."

Determine what toys you will have on hand. Make certain that these toys are safe and fit the age group that you plan to work with. VCR tapes can be purchased or rented from a local video store or library. The small rental fees are well worth having tapes on hand. Plan for extremely cold days, rainy days or days that school will not be in session.

On giving parents advice. Most will ask and welcome suggestions. They recognize your years of experience and know your track record. Tell them what you think, but it is up to them if they want to follow what you have said. Some may resent what you say. Again its best to keep these discussions one on one. Do not and I repeat do not argue with a parent. No one wins an argument and you may like to keep the business. You can always give an undesirable client notice of discontinued services. Bear in mind they signed the contract, you didn't.

Smart discipline is very important. You can't make it without it. You cannot let a child get by with an undesirable action one time and discipline him the next. Anything that is against the rules deserves attention from you. First can be a verbal warning with a brief discussion. After that than you will need to result to time outs (which takes them away from the group) or writing sentences on what they did. Remember that small children do not have a concept of time. A few minutes is very long to them. Try a minute for each year the child is of age.

As you read through the book did you take notes? Good, than you have an idea of what you need to plan. Such notes may include: making arrangements with a neighbor or planning for an emergency back up provider. They may include getting started and what your needs are. Should you have gotten too involved in reading than go back an highlight the important phrases or reread this time doing a little note taking.

Start a shelf library on various day care books for reference. There are many good books on the market pertaining to baby sitting and child care. I recommend that one take advantage of the child care information. The purpose of this book is to show one how to overcome the unusual situations that are not mentioned in other manuals. This is a cross between a self-help manual and a child care book. Following the guidelines put forth in this book you will certainly maintain a sizeable income.

Analyze any and all advice that you receive. You will learn many new objectives from others. Weigh the ideas as to use for your operation. Then decide what is best for you. It's your business, It's your call.

You definitely will not be able to please everyone. Don't try to. Henry Ford built many models of the Ford automobile, but there are many other kinds of cars made. You design your system and let the parents choose.

Take the iniative to assist parents as you are at times more familiar with procedures and can work situations out for them. One being working with the school transportation system in making arrangements for their child to board the school bus at your house. You are familiar with the phone numbers and know who to contact. Parents will appreciate this as you have saved them considerable time. Also knowing the community activities helps parents to get the children involved with gymnastics, swimming, dancing, music, turtoring, etc.

Follow the information in this book and you may make more money than you can possibly imagine. Far more than some journeyman in the trades.

Lets get going.

****

I am interested in hearing from you.
Was the information in this book useful?
What part helped you the most?
I will answer random questions?

Send inquiries to:

"Ms. Ellen"
PO Box 323
Lightfoot. Va. 23090
    or E-Mail
HowToDaycare@aol.com

MISS JANE'S
CHILDCARE
(800) 222-4444

* Transportation To and From Preschool
* Trips To Library, Pool, Park, Etc.
* Member of the Childcare Connection

JANE DOE
Anywhere, USA

BUSINESS CARD

CHILD CARE

IN MY HOME

•••

FULL-TIME
DROP-IN
BEFORE AND AFTER SCHOOL

MONDAY - FRIDAY
7:30 ~ 5:30

Accepting   ages three and up
Trips to library/park
Transportation offered to/from Preschool

ask for Jane
222-4444

Member of Child Caring Connection

•••

ADVERTISING

ABOUT THE AUTHOR

"Ms. Ellen" was born the fourth of six children. Her birth place was in a rural area of Virginia called Hyacinth. The home was not insulated, no electricity, no running water therefore no indoor plumbing.

Ellen grew up with a great imagination as a child. She and her friends played on going games of Cowboys and Indians. Where they left off in a game at the end of the day, they would continue tomorrow. Items were used for meaningful commodities, such as grains of corn for money.

She was somewhat a tomboy. At a very early age her father would take her on hunting trips. She also accompanied him on business trips to the mountains where he sold his products. She would take care of household choirs, such as bringing wood into the house for the heating and cooking stoves. She also would prepare turtles and other hunted game for family consumption.

At fifteen Ellen took a job working behind the soda counter in a country drug store. Here she saved enough money to purchase a trumpet so that she could be in the school band.

During her school years Ellen was involved in just about any activity that came along. She sang in the choir, played the trumpet in the band, acted in plays, played varsity basketball, varsity softball, and was a wild cheerleader. From these experiences Ellen remembers in detail what it was like growing up.

Later she married and started her family. At this time she moved to Norfolk, Virginia as her husband was in the military. Two children later she moved to Washington DC. There she was a resident manager of a thirty three unit apartment building.

Twins were born, so now with a total of four the family moved into a house in Rockville, Maryland. After the fifth child was born, Ellen decided to go to work to supplement the family income.Her work experiences included being a computer operator, a waitress and a cafeteria aid in the public schools.

Needing to be with her children, she decided to be a stay at home mom and started baby sitting at home. As her children got older and started leaving home the baby sitting turned into a full scale child care business.

Many people have attempted day care work and than stopped, probably for a great number of reasons. Taking care of children is almost a natural instinct for someone who has had children of their own. Even young girls learn to make extra money baby sitting a few hours at night. However it doesn't matter how good one is with children, if they are not business minded and don't know how to handle off beat situations, they most likely will give up.

Because of the need for day care operators and because Ellen has the know how, she decided to write about what it takes to be successful in the day care business.